I0554941

The Wingtip Prophecy

by Brent House

DESIGN BY THEO HALL

APRIL GLOAMING

©2023 Brent House
Design ©2023 Theo Hall

-First Edition

All rights reserved. No part of this publication may be reproduced or transmitted in
any form or by any means, electronic or mechanical, including photocopy, recording,
or any information storage or retrieval system, without permission in writing from the
publisher.

Publisher's Cataloguing-in-Publication Data

House, Brent
The wingtip prophecy / written by Brent House / design by Theo Hall
ISBN: 978-1-953932-19-8

1. Poetry: General 2. Poetry: American - General I. Title II. Author 3. Body, Mind, &
Spirit: Prophecy

Library of Congress Control Number: 2023941573

Contents

ℭ

THE SAW YEAR PROPHECIES

ℭ

THE LONGLEAF PASTORALS

℃

The Heart Pine Prophecy

℃

The Benedictory Pastoral

℃

The Saw Year Prophecies

Augur of Fired Clay

I am frail   a jar filled with moonshine.

May I rise   like vapors from a winter
morning pond   & may I turn like soil
under plow   & may I rejoice in decay
of seed in furrow   & may I sense the world like a Catahoula Cur.

I will say when I enter:

                              The land calls. The soil holds my name.

Break the jar.   Blow horns.
                              Hold with a left hand the lamp.

Right the rifle.

Augur of Deep Wells

On a land not mine I am intent to precede & search for sustenance where once my family

> axed a clearing to till
> dug down to their water.

I am baptized & I know where the depth lies for the knowledge has been passed

> through hallowed discourse.
> I walk with confidence

even in this brephic forest of second stand timber I believe to be my fellowship

> where I may take my stand
> & be swallowed in canopy.

Aunt Flannery used to say we all bound to a particular society & a particular history

> to a particular sound
> & a particular idiom.

Sometimes when I am out on this land I can hollow myself to whom I am bound to

> through sense
> through blood

& I know my blood past has taken an enemy to the water with indefeasible thirst.

> Under the waterline
> dwells redemption

in the evidence of two unyielding flows   divinity gives a hardening to the flesh

> barren thorns in the land
> deep roots in the wells.

Augur of Spike

I seen him coming

I leaned into his body as lead shattered against a backbone & he didn't break   just fell liminal

& bled   left his rumen acrid with grass & his tendons tight   a native thread   bound soil & air
                                                                    now bone-dry
                                                                    stretched slender

sharp as a fascicle of pine needles   solemn & fragile
among this red darkness of humus & imprescience   this red darkness reaved into gloaming.

I seen him breathe

then his body acquiesced in ventrine improvidence   as light through woods   falls & crosses

as a sharp blade rises   & perishes along a length of breastbone   disappears as sparks will pass
singe a wide-open bottomland   graceful as a taste of broken flesh   of winter blood
                                                                    deep & rich.

I bury my hands into the absolute & break the surface   as a pupil opens toward languish.

I seen him rising

among rutted dogwood in an evening of grazing   & gazed upon his body as a faith I sustain

in coming to wide branching country   once felled land   from this day   rising to burn crowns
rising to bear an end to shadows of darkness   rising to endue redemption from ruins

                                                  rising to mock a broken unison

rising on a gambrel with splays of beauty   so near   a red glory comes upon an uncut moon.

Augur of Ash

Among coniferous relics   magnificent & alone   skelting toward God & obscurity

I will repent fire to ash   burned   after the pine   I keep my father & testimony
                                        of arms   stretched beyond   touch kindred fingers
of hearts   sawing through ring-colored nature   & above the mantel

homage to our destruction & our mutilation of rust.

I remember some words
standing open   as covenants   & incense drifts   to wind   to glistens of needles   to sun
                                        to a salamander dry in a remnant of a puddle.

O   such a sweet savour
& time evirates hard labor   tears flesh & blains fire   wood stands asunder
                                                            O altar   alter   pour
touch a pure bone of man   separate from terrors of desire & birth   & fears of tare

myself I abhor   & mercy may recover   to stand & shade a white pillar
                                                            to make a covenant before.

I remember finding a ground rattler curled in a pile of open burrs   too cold
                                                            too slow to strike a hand
collecting kindling on a Saturday morning   & I remember

I carried it to the ditch in a wheelbarrow   or at the end of a rake   to a pile of straw
                                        it burned over a pyre   as sacrifice to our lyance

of wellkept yards & a childhood of fear   dry as fall
ran along the ground   & the stalks of bahia   came to pass

decoct to ash

spread in the chaffseed of open barrens.   Standard & poor ligatures of kudzu braids
                                        of infinite green at the pecked base of pines

shade the chastening of flames   offer a wimple defense against fire.

No succor shall strong winds provide   & plentiful wealth conspires
                                                with a vestige of laying fascicles

retainers of a season to scorch & wilt the vine that round a native birth runs
to glean trouble as surely as sparks fly upward   & to consume even among the thorns.

Augur of Pines

What we have left is a glory of pine limned to give way
verecund   stands of limbs   lost to make way.

So sap will seep & what is done is done.

How sharp are the labors of comeuppance
the gnaws of scions usufruct.

As good will foible right we pray against evil   we seek to avert by the virgin
forests of longleaf pine.

For our way to the sovereign hearth   tenures upon the land.   Verily the barrow
sacrifices in vain.

Can I only take courage   for the divine is divine   the line a heavenly lineage.

An uncle unknown to me was born of timber. The son of a widow & an itinerant
who came & clear cut through. Leaving us to just wonder
& mayhap see as we never seen before
a glory in royal company.

An undying race moves now & forever more in a shadow world
undone   in a vast & wrought vision
nature gives blood to rings of veins.

Above   stars & moon shine
a common boon
a common boon
a common boon.

Glories dwell not in a while of light ebbing & flowing to bygones ashes & complines.
Such lese-majesty endured by a man who dwells not in the shelter of most high pines.

Our own should recognize all their works of bygone might & bygone beauty & disparage
not to acknowledge our name

& we should accolade our errant blood with resinous blazons of lightered.

An array of arms in light
& knotty remnants of a tale once told   settled in a legitimate line
born country of akerning.

Keloid

I turn shibboleth to ruin unity. I see a dimly shining history opening a soft pulp of throats.

Rose cones in pastures of beaten gold found by a seersage of the throng & murmured past the life men love

births splendours of demesne.

A vast opening.

Fine & duly impressed to cast their lot:
        Hintons Cuevases Rouses Pentons Jones McDonalds Lees Stockstills
        Davises Landrums Jordans Bakers Crosbys Sherrills Ladners Slades
        Moores Grahams Thompsons Byrds McNeills Coxes Shaws Freemans
                                        & brood away in the flaming sun.

Augur of Principle

Land Lord.

The broken door unseams to rejoice in the hinges.

Upon hearing

as mortars gain from crumbs.

Sweet

the blood & body

where a prophet is

& I have no carpentering belt

only faith genuflected before a return.

In the exchange of resurrection

so the hammer

lands on the charge.

Augur of Flailing

The mantic threnody of the mockingbird   mourned from a plum branch

                                           a cruel hope passing

a cruel boy pointing at exposures of white breast

                                              & resounding strange fruit

his copper seeds arching imperfect   through the air

                                    eyes following a slow progression.

Lord   I lament   quail with remorse of intransigent sin

                                  & touch light still flailing by reverbs

damp is the hole from which I pluck the bead

                                  the chamber ruddles with shot return

a body held quivers with terrene blood.

Lord   you mistake me much   I lament this medley

                                  so dueled by asperity & carry such

parabolic loss in scaphoid palms

                                meager penance for an arbitrary disgrace

encloses true resonance

                            in rooted soil I wail clods into wrenching veins.

Augur of Wright

Sorghum pours drone through an assurance of pipes
                                to quell a rally of sympathy

& a Mississippi child wants music flowing
                                sweet as stamen incised
                                from honeysuckle & wisteria

petals pestled into morning robes of resurrection
                                come down from the hill.

A memory of a simple cottage gone from the square
                                restored by the gifts
                                of a hand-carved chancel

a window of old English glass & a new roof
                                inverted by shipmakers

& walls of beaded boards filled with remains
                                of elders transformed.

Such great loss & relative little evidence
                                dents in the hardwood
                                an overseer dead

dead in a let him save himself March
                                what so rose in December
                                only fragrant memory

in June when the gulf reaches to the lake once more
                                when mentors pass a smoldering
                                over the river & marred passes.

Augur of Shibboleth

Some words will not roll off my tongue   like Massachusetts
so   in Vicksburg cannon fire formerly spoke through the branches

& when I went up those rolling hills & saw the stones bearing names I said
                              Daddy   we killed a bunch of mass a two shits.

The skeleton of a sunken gunship was waiting reconstruction. Timbers alive in the river
                                        held a new
                                        vicinage
                                        preserved
                                        under mist
for we burned our cotton bales on the banks at night.

Along the fencerows mother cursed the miracle trees sawed to cord

through the bight & laches of her tongue   so

I grew to worship thaumaturgic wood   egrets & mockingbirds dropped
                              along barbed strands stretched above the ground

& still crepe myrtle fell to an immuring need for ordonnance. Timber   pulp of my flesh
                                        fell across hills

sibilant in fervent air

as the land lined with creosote posts   black & tarry resinate.

Augur of Illuminated Manuscript

Puncture turned to tear

the pull of my father's arm

on the ream of wire

steel unstrands across a line

field with the smoothness of vellum

frail into the hard-red clay

staple into blackened posts

leather of glove worn

in the curl of grip

taut then tie wire to corner

fabric of his shirt dries

on a nail embedded

run threads through

the sloping manuscript of hills

This will be here long after I'm gone.

Augur of Resonant Woods

Sound carries through woods

without tears of body hindering

release of air bound under

the ancient roots core of an emptiness

surrounded as gardens in forest.

Soil blesses tomato plants with scion

promises to pulp from toil

in swelter of early morning

a glistening

with a weight of journey.

Wafting through narrow

rows of produce by stray grasses

the soft vibrations of a cavity

filling as bushels bound for market.

These morning notes

so gently carry

the bounding of prayers.

Augur of Begottenness

Touch me not until my hands are washed in transcendence.

The peelings of skin in the market of veined fruits do not subvert the richness of my soil
or alter courses & calls of a minister who knows not sin
but the gifts of tomato okra & squash.

My garden is abundant with symmetry.

A line of growth will not be broken even as the clods untilled.

I have weaned the sucking shoots from the branches so this produce may be laden
beyond a season.

My soil is rich
cakes upon my hands & gloves would yield me barren so let us be patient for the drying.

Augur of Tendrils

These tendrils come upon you as a sign   such hemorrhages of vine gather on the wood

long after seeds are planted & gathered in soft blankets
                                                          my heart bruits with abundant murmurs

across clarities of hunger   thirst   nakedness & heavy iron yokes
                                                          gather until tears swelt upon root

crowns laid in antiquated railbeds   gather like an invasion of panicles   like soil of far lands

done brought against soil from near   soil whose tongue   you do not understand.

In your high concept of your fierce countenance   you favor the fruit of your land
                                                          & you will eat your monotony

away   behind gates   until high & spireful pines come down   as shadows
in lands you have trusted.

These tendrils shall reach until no light can be found

beneath the old growth   besiege a land of discernment   intent fruit of our body

shall absorb a sober pain   shall bury ground held by blood   & in their straightness

pine shall distress with a tender & delicate path

shall leave a remnant   shall spread when nothing is left   shall clutch ground

& though few in number   their taproots spread beyond hot

humid summers & soft falling rains   & you shall be left to nought   but rejoice

for I am scattered across the land   plucked from the wind   & I possess a trembling heart.

Augur of Forest for Trees

A jubilee of tolerance   scars the share of stock & hardy

tracks over trestles of a bonanza fading   I

watch past   I could not see working now

as I retire into a pine canyon   of comment & dogwood

blooms with drops of blood   crossing to unceasing

& full of glorious bands   expanding outward

to the knots of petrify in the soil   base & accumulate

until chains of a father farmer   bound from the muck

of lowlands   recompense for the statant.

Augur of Bare Scars

Aleatory bloom   deepen each fall to germination   & Lord
rouse scars bared   the beautiful lace upon.

Doyenne
I walk on a path of fire & erudition. I pass a gentleman.

He is empathy & I carry his cross   his heritage.

So behold   confederations of a forest come mediating between mine & arbitrations of
                                                                          savage
                                                                          courage

& a skein of apocryphal yarns is darkening the horizon with a quest for prey
                                        by the buoyant rigors of a grisly fire.

They have survived fires & storms. The bark on those trees is fire
                        but they bare the scars. I have often thought

they sure would sheath their bold innards in an aggregate of leaves
                                        now hollow claims an early sake.

So I don't think we can seep the righteousness of calloused sap.

Yet Almighty God Lord of heaven & earth   we beseech thee to pour forth thy blessing
upon this land & to give us a fruitful season   that we constantly receive thy bounty
                                                     may evermore give thanks unto thee.

For this bounty is an ordinance of enmity to my flesh   a pestilence to set my face against.

For a fall shall pursue   sounds of a shaken leaf shall cause a sward to atrophy
                                in fields of raw joy & dung hist by heaps of panegyric
                                                                          indigence.

For a mere pyre of hoven fuel   a cloven plain I will not cast away   nor shall I abhor
& utterly destroy   nor shall I break my covenant

but I shall mark this bounds as an instance stands   as transcendence toward baseness
                                                inhumanity with scant sympathy.

Behold   I am recklessly in no place   listening to the backwoods flaunt their poverty
revel unashamed & richly articulate   & this is still my country   holding lucid scars
reaped & sown.

Days come a darkness & consecration.

Doyenne
I will not abnegate my empyreal bloodline for your fears
                                                        & yapping of hounds from dusk to debouch.

Behold   waters come from a far country   & the reproaches of a fecund land cover
                                                                        as the sky tresses.

Arisen is red clover crushed   before
like streams in the hollows   pass

go nowhere & perish.
Provide no atonement.

Behold   I stumble through a sedulous portion.

A lack of civility is licking the dust   & a soil becomes man
                                                        except of the breath.

What is done in the soil does not remain in the soil   comes to the sun.

Sometimes I get so tired of relenting to foments of forests.

This world's a wilderness of woe.   Where shall I go.
                                                        O where shall I go.

I bound to go to a wilderness of weeps & moans.
By the grace of God I'll carry on.

Share my coffle.   You can hinder me here
                                                        & you can't hinder me there.

See the manifestation of my produce.   You don't know about high fall fields.
How blood is invigorated.

I'll tell you the truth.

My blood done been laden by history   & distance shall be.
From a stand along a trace watchers come   from a far country   & reproach covers.

Doyenne   you shall be given no reddition from the coffers of my bone   & a mound of ash
                                                              from frail white trash
                                                              will be blown against hope.

Still the pale palliative may persist among the emanations of trees
                              & stark is the constant sorrow springing from man's enclave.
                              This is a cloud over a hinterland of quagmire & permeation.

Scar   behold   country   god   soil.   Fear from fealty of our caterwaul.

The rolling hills are bound among us like dog day's summer rain   springing homesteads.

A sharecropper named Page on Uncle Joe's place left after one summer
the house cut from longleaf yellow pine   empty as the stagnant swamps of shiners & bluetick.

I'm thinking he yoked together an ox & an ass   but you read that can't be done
in Deuteronomy   & the blessings of penury.

Doyenne   our agon ain't laid with aught remit   we ain't to be no mendicant stumps
in some miasma. Our land will so long languish & the refrains of the juba
                                        lay in the soil as the tree rose to be cut.

The blade will break the soil in tribute   & the sun braid upon the etiolate.

Behold   the ken of the pale face of clouds.   A storm is coming I'm afraid
& it looks to me like a dredging of sky
like a troubling done baring down
like a place you wouldn't tarry

& this is still my country   even though the devisal of horizon through blood shatters me
& I am a wavering by an honor near salvers   pride near spittoons.

Behold   loss.

Yet Almighty God   I pray the recollection of it will remain with me as unfailing
consolation will remain after I have experienced what I in a certain sense dread
more than the thunderstorm   although I am indebted to your generosity
                                                              for its coming
secessions of rills from many glacis.

So many of our hills turn sage in the fall   for the soil is too acidic   in need of bone.

We are a fragile & brittle brokenness yearning to the hollow benison.

20

Once I shot this squirrel down from a tree. I went to pick it up & it bit into my finger & God have mercy it hurt me. I thought I wasn't ever gonna get that thing off either.

Tell you what though
I got that squirrel dressed & soaked it in vinegar
to take out the wild taste   if you didn't know.
It made a good stew.

Still got them marks. I tell you that squirrel left a tatting on me.

Doyenne   you ain't from around my neck of the woods.
My kin wouldn't think you got enough sense to come in from the rain.

I do.

Behold   a rheumy pine.

Augur of Knowledge

Equally strong are the tempered blade & the resinous wood

& though the wood brings forth its sap in a fragrant pause

the blade is broken   cast into rust of labors   a remnant

as a fear that won't fade away   but still remembers

how the fluids can accumulate   within a body

remembers how the fragile fig   both limb & fruit

seeps sweet   among the foliage   a blessing

& just before   there appears a crop of small knobs

not the real figs   but a kind of forerunner

& they are eaten by the hungry

they come to their own indefinite maturity

& they fall   enter the soil like flakes of rust

like a warming bond   into disintegration

an elemental contact   with an illusion of separation

but water   fallows the field   washes into the cut soil

& cleans the bleeding   wood gathers in valleys

of barn roofs   & pours onto the assemblage

of brokenness   blades & tools   corrosion

gathers brittle & decayed

& under a harbinger   leaves deeply lobed flesh

open to a pine heart rose.

Augur of Bough

So genuflect neither will I   though you may pour white sin upon

my arms will not break   but will fall to earth   & frill the soil

with whorlings of resinous pulp

will offer exudations   amber drops   in the décolleté of roots

as an oil of joy for mourning   an incubus of heaviness

I praise

garment of needles   called righteousness

the planting of the Lord   glorified in the seeds   risen

to stand among high places
to stand among falling

so genuflect neither will I   though these hills become a home

worn smooth with hunger.

Augur of Cleavage

Ain't you all just a little too high & mighty here
                                          with your two dollar sins & scripted wine
                                                          & your inerrant lies

I'll tell you
your beloved son said he wasn't gonna get all haughty   but he meant not right now

just one day when he got a little money in his pocket   I'll tell you   he's gonna throw
                                                      a brick through your stained glass
                                                      & head up where those horses run

I'll tell you
those eyes done been looking off between the high hills   like they done seen some pass
& now you might as well keep your eyes on those rocks

because the whittled staff is gonna rise
& split them until they flow with blood & water   & honey
                                                                            & milk

& a stone shall be placed on the tongue of my firstborn son
                                    until it shall quiver with life as a risenpore

I tell you his flesh will weigh & heave your soul upon rocks
                                              with your beloved son gone
                                                  & soughed in the air
                                                      as wheat blown
                                                          & chaff fall

just one day of sustenance will pass
hunger will sanctify the righteous   voice of my son
tables will be set with challah   a sweet braid not easily broken

you will find a house born of flesh
& his palms will hold envious mountains
where silver will be cast away & a zealous suitor   tears the curtain

for the temple ain't long for pharisaic law
ain't long to be made vile by eye & bud

I tell you this truth

a son will be born too poor & noble   & his tongue will pulse under the rocks of your flesh
                                              & he will eat judgment through your breasts
                                                    with a blade of jagged love.

The Longleaf
Pastorals

Pastoral [So great a debtor]

So great a debtor I am obliged to be   & needing redemption   from rusted barbs of strung
                                                                            wire I climb

as a stranger who will wander   & follow deep ruts of cattle through clearings & pine
                                                                            his stray path

will come to a house   built upon sand   near a creek where springs flow to ever bless
                                                                            spanish moss

reach arms to ground   & tune ears to grace   as streams of water offer purest praise
                                                                            I kneel & drink

until I cease   & water becomes a voice   melodious   & falling onto flaming tongues
                                                                            burned spirits

of sin   I inherit   & I am burdened with despair   & I bleed from the fold of God as flesh
                                                                            held in fetters

I wash prone in these waters   carry my body down to the creek   called after Hickory wood
                                                                            fallen & hand

scraped into a native floor   I am asleep upon & coming to a house   I claim with my blood.

Pastoral [The violence of lightning strking pine]

The violence of lightning striking pine   downright pastoral in present time
as generations gather on front
porches to watch rain end

steam rise from the asphalt   & prismatic remnants fall   from fasciculus needles
my father always told me
lightning gathers

around the edge of clouds   so watch   don't get caught in an open cab when a storm comes
I've seen red bark peel
crown to root

seen stately pines splinter into pulp   as branches spread to strike twice
gold bright as northern bowers
& bury deep into soil

depths below ashes   sawdust   songs a mockingbird perched in uppermost limbs
even the hawk must abandon
his lofty perch

as charges descend to devour a heart   besiege a towering spire   at the edge of the canopy
topple groundward
as horizon

tears toward the earth   startlingly   loud as peals of thunder roll   a second   third
& fourth pulse hotter than sun
viscous is the gap

between softwood & bark   as sap runs through the trunk   heats to gas   expands   explodes
tears deep into the bole.

Pastoral [So cast back to an old place]

So cast back to an old place   moss changed
                                                                    & I'd like to hope

there some awakening down the way   an absolution of chattels
to echo through hollows   in a scarcity of stays

& springs in locked babbles arose of undermining endeavors to blur a reflection.

Once there was a house of lapboard here   but it's gone. I come a long way down
the road.   Past a grass widow in bandore.

So mourn   my boon friend   a hole on the earth   a privileged place of origin
                                                               haven attuned divination

We can claim ours is a shallow pool. God reigns on the dust & the unjust.

Exodus: God of Moses   parted a Red Sea   in a continuous cycle of relatively autonomous
but interlocked moments   long gone & in a hurry.   Moses lacked elocutionary movements
pitch force   abruptness & time   & reeds brake.

O   we flow down to the creek   ceded & granted   & we are drunk
                              & whoso drinks of the living water will thirst no more.

So pour me   here in a darkness   by strength of water
as a fine twilled fabric of silk & worsted   & crepe.

Who can tell the extent of each movement without bearing witness to the gestures of each
                                                               mourning passion?

I'd like to hope   inherent capacities would not be encompassed.   I'd like to hope
opposition would spring   against a dominant way.

   I'd like to hope our structures could not be bound. I'd like to hope some extra will be sown.

                         I distill to a hundred proof & pass over rye.

There are empty rooms in a house of yellow pine lapboard   I know.

I'd saunter on up there
if it weren't for time   & I don't hold nothing in me   cause all that wrong gotta be rightened

                                        I speck   to lay down in a sanctified bosom
                                            shore bound & cast so wistful.

So we flow down from the old place right into Hickory   to Pearl   to our Gulf
                                              to an origin of circulation
                                                I'd return to avoid.

Come   quench by living water below field's life.

So strengthen limbs hanging down   & feeble knees
    & make straight paths   so what is lame may be healed   lest to fall short of the graces of God
                                            lest any root of bitterness spring up
                                              lest any profane like Esau   who
for one morsel sold a birthright & rejected his blessing of inheritance & repents
                                            by shores of diligent tears.

It is not a simple thing the ground swells to pore.

To bloodshed behind a house   these scourges skin
& bone embodiment of an underlying faithshed.

God: the years of relative neglect
then took a shine.

I drink of the water of my ancestors.

I am drawn clear across.

I come to a wellspring.

Pastoral [I always find myself over yonder]

I always find myself over yonder on my side of the river   close to home

because I saw no need for gallivanting & knew my source well

my antediluvian fallings have amerced me under leaking roofs of red

& rust nestled into hay tight with thwarted fermentation

joined with genteel grasses & lain me with scythed bodies

effaced fields of early summer

breathed bare presence in the full storehouse of my father's heaven

holed down into the darkness of locked stacks   loosened strings

bound ententes   fortified in a common ancestry

                                  grown incalescent in ardent isolation.

I am alone   in my retinue of loss

until the mockingbird makes an easy nest   under rafters loaded   with warmness

until ground slackens   & embraces ankles   until the fall rains

have pulled the herd from low stubble of permanent pasture

until two snakes shed perfect skins in my quiescent loft   until God takes peccable eyes

& soils   until winter perseveres upon my enclave & bales fall

to consumption   & rains fall on a bare concrete floor.

I fall to labor in fields unknown

until the slats of the hayrack swell smitten with first cuttings

vain offerings of comely & manifest provisions

until my bliss is a floor strewn with haystraw

                            & blood falls from strings cut into bare hands.

Pastoral [Amen rises amid pales]

Amen rises amid pales   splits wood as a bay when a quest been found & carries light to
dark

        & light again

waits for ardent tongues to edify a formicary & quake with accent rhythm & intonation

as amen rises a life of needles joined haphazardly emerges as language.

        I cannot speak

cannot join either by revelation by knowledge by prophecy or by doctrine

as I am spelt in plain interpretation & will not break root truth for fervent affection

        & I war with the swyke

        that feir ant freoly ys to fyke

who comes through denses of canebrake through treelines & through fields heavy grazed

rising mounds of clay for he is endowed by power of bite & sting

        a second blessing of venom

as a hoard of workers secure privative waters wash a triune body buried & risen again.

I migrate to mind devour as an instar rising above roots & lay safe in a thin state of grace

in a bramble bed in an open pasture lined with myrtle oak & pine & I listen to communion

to spirit baptism to faith so uttered the divine becomes man

        flesh pierced with conception.

Pastoral [This entire most beautiful order]

This entire most beautiful order of good things is going to pass

                        after its measure is made & been exhausted.

I stoop in my weakness to reveal supernumerary shoots of stem

                        pinch away & root in adventitious seasons.

Take away growth rich from decay of boarded mounts   sawdust

                  as life varied & untruly immense must take most vital guidance.

In such rich loam indeterminate stalks grow in need of suckering

                    an intimate disjoint at the axil enjoins a bequested succor.

The fruit of the vine is entirely a matter of mercy   revelation

                       weans gentle from earth   makes most vital obeisance.

Pastoral [Saplings fall under axe]

Saplings fall under axe

& pat fire gone awry from origins in harvest field

& chaff toward & across barbed

wire it will not be long until the forestry

men come & steer ditchdiggers through

this mass of trees & tomorrow

in the tar brought to the blackened

bark of old growth remains

& the char of sage & fallen needles

stitching the floor.

Pastoral [Hunger raddles]

Hunger raddles the body & above tree lined pastures   open gauges

consume memory as an afterbirth full of nutrients
& black shadows fall in circles of stagnant horizon

as a communal body in the sky waits & last breaths push against

an empty body fallen to the ground
mercifully lost in a bed of humus

so much mercy is not unknown or forgotten in a prodigal & savage land

on sweet birch & swamp maple
buzzards perch in insolent readiness

ravishing & turbulent   bent into a lowing pain   lo & behold

they stand on high branches & seize darkness
break from the shoulder   heavy   born remnants

& talons bring salvation from perishing   as evenfall would bring   coyotes from hills far away

hanging on a tree line   as death humbles the head   even of born predators

of terrible eyes
of floppy tongue
of outstretched limbs
of hooves soft from the belly.

Pastoral [Glorious body drawn from fields]

Glorious body drawn from fields   through a gate
& a mouth of disaster   red with a rural irony   a chute

a body pressed into a cage   rusted & shitted   bound toward Poplarville
on a highway past Juniper Grove   where small men return to poor soil

to the days of tin haze & abundance   yards
crops of flesh   green fed & scour stained   in dirt pens

consumed   & once a rotten slat of floor gave   ground away
legs
                                                     & a habit of acres

gone   & the cold of the slaughter house

& yet a brindled heifer

too tall for an Angus field bull   opens a sale barn door   her horns whetted sharp
                                          as drovers cower
                                        buyer boots displace
                                  & the auctioneer stutters

a wild one

no man on the front row will place her on his card & no offers to carry her into a silver bed
                                               & so withdrawn

wide pastures draw nigh.

Pastoral [Among bales I crawl]

Among bales I crawl   through bahia & rye   breathing the evening dust through
                                                long bores of clarity   open sky

I fear not   nothing   raised up by four corners of a common evil   & a weight of cold

I fear nothing   not torments of hope   nor the thing with feathers that perches in the soul
                                          leaves remnants   pelt & bone   I fear not

because I know no one puts new cut hay in old barns   as new cut hay bursts into fire
                                                            & old barns ruin

so new cut hay must be cured in pasture   must suffer   shed life & hope   must be put away

hazy for breath   I crawl in a dry winter of loose stubble   & a crack of sheath
                                              moults   under a rough cut joist

I fear not the remnant of this other   coming to crawl from its skin.

Pastoral [Amidst ashes]

Amidst ashes my father burns limbs   in a deep bed of remnant woods

                                             in timbered tracks of a dummy line

he plows ash to soil   until a deep gash settles to mute a history of theft

                                        & his wife tells me all her family is dead

her truth   thin as venous blood   falls in licent fields of her deeds

                                           & still a procreant urge of the world

through the leaves of grass & seethe

        & seethe a feeble mind with fear of its close   but the soil lives   & blessed be my soil

let the soil of my salvation be exalted

for it is soil that avenges & subdues its people

for it is soil that loves   & hates   & is eaten by worms

                                     that is lost & rises hard toward brokenness
                                     & gives inches of rising to cover our fall.

Pastoral [We threw roots into fire]

We threw roots into fire until we were derelict   ash & dust   memory of a begotten trough
                                                                                                                                  filled with the spirit

& skeps of char   until our intarissable woods exhaust into an advent   pasture's guild
                                                                                                                                  understory remnants

once covered with old growth   & then cut away   circles of time widened on carse
                                                                                                                                  narrowed on hill

the native sadness tracked   until shotguns & dogtrots came   & kept fast unto a sustenance
                                                                                                                                  deep & hard faith

until desire removed the pith   & ploughed   with jagged blades of blood & tars
                                                                                                                                  hot with release
                                                                                                                                  & so long kept

a husband & a son without a title to land   so the absent whelp of an intemperate memory
                                                                                                                                  claimed the maternal soil

the fields so diligently crafted   in the tracks of the dummy line that led our fathers   here
                                                                                                                                  to pines now lost.

Pastoral [A stubborn roan lows]

A stubborn roan lows in a minor key   in memory of hunger   carried through winter
                                                              petitions to honorable pines
                                                                   a great brood suffers
                                                                     O dolorous sound

high lonesomeness roots & sad omens of her furious hope & breath ruthless as red corral
                                                                wide slats against the field

wither as a plot without shadow of a cloud   as a yearling coft
                                                         extilled upon inheritance I accouche
                                                             so the song of silence is still

all good times past & gone & once forlorn in burlap   our folk engross in entrails
                                                                 as the flies green into never
                                                                    & the driving shuffle
                                                                         beat of blood

flows like milk on sand   strains through glass & tears our aural tapestry
                                                                 & her broadside a crown
                                                                       of tailbone I rest
                                                                          my chin upon

I roll my sleeves & bear our deep intimacy in a gird of nuzzle   run headlong
to my own ruin   hold bones against red wood   & our hollow waters descend
                                                         & unfold flesh in labor & firstborn locked
                                                             in a working chute or a raincut furrow
                                                                among lumber & ruff of hoof
                                                                  or   fallen & broken stubble

O blue tongued flow plight of troth   vein-striped sack   harrowed body
                                                                 O constant sorrow I seen trouble
                                                                      & I ought of known

when I seen her go away back on the other side of the hill   where rain lingers
                                                                    on blanched white bone
                                                                      & fallen down pine

she lays in the straw bellows amid loneliness kicks against her ribs
                                              pushes to a threshold as imminence stalls in passage hips lock
                                                         & birth should not struggle   should swell udders
                                                                  & flow water from the cracks

42

& should resonate the head cradled under the tense hoop   & when birth does not
I have bared arms   have pulled flesh from flesh   worn gloves to my shoulders
                                        & pulled until shit rolled down
                                              tied ropes from a winch

& still birth does not come   & the body lays asyen   O how can I tell of a tongue now dry
                                                    & cleaving to the jaw

O thou that inhabitest

O how can I tell of the divelled body   I cross cut to bone

                                        thou didst not deliver

thou art taken out of the womb & thou didst make me hope upon a mother's nipple
                              upon frets I cast my fingers & pick the guts strung
                                        & not far from constant sorrow

for there is none to help   only strong Angus bulls   beset & gape as they pour out like water
                      all his bones come out of joint   his heart melts in the midst of his bowels
                                        & the chrism of his blood falls in poral soil

& it causes me to tremble as I shroud him in gunny sack
                                        & save the cleft ribbons of flesh
                                        & save the long whip of his tail

as none can save his own soul   none can pleck the frailing root note
                                    so I will graft upon the venal fullness of her milk
I will graft a remnant   will redress a hunger   with scents of redemption

of piation for the gentle Holstein   his white & black held at bay by a suffusion of hide   kithe
                                                    bear witness

she will smell only loss & blood   upon his shoulder he will bear

she will suffer him come as joint heir   will fain over his swounding helplessness

when I rope fresh hide on that calf & pen him under the weight of death
& his precocial legs   I hope nothing more   than they should share this woe
                                        share hope & each live in expectation

amidst a bed of hay & hazy dust
share resonance of tight cords on a frame laid as a foundation of the world

                                            & heel bound
                                            I still wonder

as hot beest comes to pass   to this rightness to orphan born.

Pastoral [In the bright falling]

In the bright falling of the devil beating his wife

earth is imputed by sky & drought
brought

replete with sad & tender grace & passionate regret
for the hills & branches & trees & powerful grasses

I ferment in guilt fused in ambient air

lie in acknowledgement
far away within foreknew

some shall reap

equitable punishment of labor justified by places
primogeniture

remove all sights that our eyes have gazed upon
& forgive a righteous settlement

mournful as a rainbow over sorrow's pasture

the increase fallen & gone for good
as the deep sky surges

all my outdoor work is left unfinished
& past fields lament.

Pastoral [O fall down barn]

O fall down barn   O Heav'n please stand just a little while longer

        remember how he poured his salt & blood into your veins
        remember your roots
        remember how longleaf stood transfixed by gulf water
        remember him through our drought

offer abasht children a thin ring from your poles & throw down roots from your beams
from the rods atop your rafters bring light & from your roistered vein
        point our direction true south

O fall down barn

let me lose every appendage in your loft for I am prideful & my word is hollow

O hallowed barn   rot into flesh engrain pores for your resin is holy fire

I will strike the lintelpost   & you will humble for your promise is just as mortise & tenor
        & cannot be broken

in high winds & scarce water I speak to the well & waters flow like a deluge
        for your promise is just

I stand in awe & in hunger
I offer my son & daughter to lay under the bright sky

to lay under the wide gates we have hoisted to the beams
to lay unheled & be pierced among the bright shafts of red nail light

to carry splinters of your truth so deep under their kin
no blade will dig away their holy presence

O fall down barn
I pray blood into love of this timber I cry out & you must hear

O fall down barn how dare you lean down this hill when I cry

for I ain't nothing   you hold all which is beautiful
        wild & ain't nothing domestic can lay
under your wood   hay of our beds dead & bound smells of field
        staves of feedtrough hold remnant of molasses

O fall down barn   red up your wall   before your gray planks loam into soil
                                             in the hereness of water & air

before my eyes   you are rusticated   through rust & ruth
                       when once you sat in the square & lifted your gambrels into afternoon
                                                 black as a red wingtip

when once I slept in the heart of barnés   as a child of royal gumption & comeuppance

O   had I known afore I know now   I fear I should not have had heart enough
                       though you will no longer remember & somebody should
                                          & somebody should remember

& somebody should remember

as water drains through a screen   a mat of pulp even lays down in a press & dries
                       on the brittle sound of just chapiters   we lay in substantial exposure

we lie & we wrinkle in the rain & we curl in the sun
& when we ignite anointed as leaves

as red checkered pride   as purple leaft resurrection   we ignite to feed soil   as rich milled
woven fibre laid down   pressed   & dried to feed hunger days   dry of press & pulp

& if you wrap my body in burlaps of sackcloth

I will be your liveral fautor   will be ground to dust   & will ascend the way of rough earth
& yellow-eyed   to lofts of fairheaded whither
                                          & lofts of handworked mystery

O fall down barn   tin folded pine   fallen into good ground & brought

forth   old tin of fruitfulness   I hath forsaken brethren   sistern   father   mother   wife
                                          for son   & daughter   & our land

for this persecution of inheritance   an hundredfold   some sixtyfold   some thirtyfold
                                                       & everlasting

O fall down barn   spring up & bare.

Pastoral [On hazy mornings]

1. Cutting

On hazy mornings diesel funnels amber & blue through spouts bound by nylon stockings
blade shafts are greased
points of light ricochet through nail holes in the tin
the plow is put on the tractor's three-point hitch: left   right   then center.

There is rye to be planted   a winter green that scours the herd if hay runs short.

Dew holds the field.

Then   in the dryness   dust crowds the air.

Summer rust scrapes the ground.

Sweat   dirt & sun   grasp arms   neck   ears   darken flesh   into a farmer's tan.

Cypress weeds   crabgrass   thick white roots fall into skewed rows as the hoof-packed ground
gives to the blades.

2. Planting

After the powdering of soil black with decay & years of erosion
bound for this ground
seeds must be strewn for winter graze
to be life in the midst of moving away from the sun.

The rye is thrown a winter green that will scour the herd when hay runs short.

Pallets hold the sacks. Then each is emptied into the spreader
the strings of closure pulled away   fine seeds among pellets of nitrogen   phosphate   potash.

I take my path across the field   watching the flight of seed released   so the falling
will not reach past   but touch.

3. Grazing

So the forage is gone from summer pastures   stalks abandoned to deeper hunger
the grass is grown   bearing a fall of wet soil that gives under hoof.

The rye has grown   a winter green that scours the herd as hay runs short.

Chains hold the gate. Then   with the ground finally dry & firm   the hinges creak
I stand aside   as the warmth of the herd passes onto new ground.

Far afield they will ramble   though the green is as deep here as the ridge past the hollow.

Pastoral [Falling among beams]

Falling among beams like mercy is the illusion of unity   & a famine of desire   dry

> *beams of light fall*   *a yield of dream*

desacralising breasts from bone   ripples like a skin of jubilee held in running water

> *carnal bodies*   *passing over seeds*

under sand   ripples like betrayal & how can I not cleave to hills   as honey

> *near river headwaters*   *winding a way through hills*

discords from the suckle high on the cleft   as detritus in the foam   floats to a sandbar

dead still   like a strong will   like a fogginess that neither sinks nor swims   neither

opens to the pull of current   nor ravels from a cut off   & the red opening of an equal pair
                                        opening of a red heart

> *seed between*   *sweet & veined*

scars like a broken bottle embedded in mud   beaten smooth as feet bottoms eagerly

follow the path of abrasions   to dark pools   churning with leaves   live   but a minute
                            or how long the flesh is able to hold   below the water.

Pastoral [Deep within the ravine]

Deep within the ravine   a maternal low raises constant   & resonant as diesel engines
                                                        turbines kicking like legs buried
in quicksand   & the flesh of birth dilates like the eyes of a cow held in conveyer belts
                                                        being wenched upward
& dropping life into the giving ground as her body raises   necessary & inevitable

& I can imagine if this calf is a heifer we'll name her Sandy
                                                        because we are that kind of people

the kind of people who name our few cattle roaming these less than a thousand hills
                                                        & we are the kind of people

who think of our cattle as part of our whole   & son   you'll starve before those cows.
                                                        We are the kind of people

who count each head as it passes between fields & know good & well
                                                        when one is missing from the herd

& we are the kind of people who persist   & we are the kind of people who find
                                                        deep within the ravine

the fallen body

& rejoice in the coming labor.

Pastoral [God must rather bushhog]

God must rather bushhog than disc
                              I'm thinking
cause always when I'm bushhogging
                              there comes a point of trinity
where the tractor swings a wide
                              triad of cones to cut
to a final swath of Bahia.

Discing is row after row
                              like the Pharisees & Sadducees
so carefully cut beyond thinking
                              rolling a skin of Earth before
sin & the erosion thereof.

Like rain would be dew
                              in Eden but
there's either too much or not enough.
                              I read
in the *Progressive Farmer* the other day
                              it rained
seventy-four inches in one day
                              on Cilaos.

Things like that ought not happen
                              I'm thinking
though I honestly can't say I know
                              much about Cilaos
but here there's flights of puffweed
                              washing of solums.

The Heart Pine Prophecy

The Heart Pine Prophecy

Stars falling after still giving birth to a path of broken glass stained for future egression.
I am trembled & not afraid.

God: such a galumph yet to follow a sign of welkin to replete   a languid knowledge
to clear across a roiling land
to see among turbid mores.

Lord: I am beholden
above all.

Trampled on the ground & fallen as nature created a bona fide recklessness
anent powers given tatterdemalion men who howl & wail
in grief & in jubilation of penetrable wisdom & wealth.

A journey to needs.

All I must for this journey is stilled in a small country where my relations are.   Too long
have I laid insouciant in my safe house steepled by timbers of glory & worship.

I won't say it's not a hard thing to say fare thee well to my country
but when I get lonely   I'll sit down & cry.   I'll just sit down & cry.

I tell you so my joy may be in journey & my journey may be complete.
Yet maundering through.
How roods lie upon ways.

One of my brothers told me to hold faith in my destination drawing nigh & wash my hands.

One of my uncles told my father he'd give him twenty dollars or twenty acres if he'd vote
a couple times for county supervisor & that was back when twenty dollars & twenty acres
was the same   & they ain't now
but what did he know

didn't know the extant land
didn't divine with the entrails of a sacrificial animal
didn't bring the susurration of God to my ears & permeable feet.

For mine   an extensive land anciently rich & thriving now greatly wasted & destitute.

All through this world I'm bound to wander:

In the dark hills of blood   velvet moss   myth   fear   loss   bleeding armadillos   mélanges
banks of streams   magnolias   mossy oaks   clapboard   neutra rats   ponds   big chaws
mutts   raccoons   creek bottoms   bait plots   buck & doe   spotted fawn   double aught
gralloch   skinned hides   yaps & yelps   drizzle   yonder   springwood   poison oak
poison ivy   flooded gulleys   mites   buzzards   gently rolling hills   alluvial clay   live oak
longleaf yellow pine   bark   Catahoula Cur   baying   pine needles   fencelines   ditches
country miles   single wides & double wides   forest fires   slopes   starkly vertical barrens
massive oaks   sandy loamy topsoils   hard clay   subsistence   poverty   dogtrot cabins
seeded windowsills   bare wood floors   battlefields   corn cribs   rail fences   epic plundering
local tradition   sawmills & turpentine kilns   taps   resin   lightered knots   ball lightning
eyeblinks   ghosts   lightning bugs in Mason jars   south facing monuments   bona fides
old-timers   acres   roosters & hens   red wheelbarrows   straining   dragging   utterly laid bare
privation   loblolly pines   strays   wherewithal   straw   free-ranging herds   holiness   hollows
rickety stands   brainches   thin white bay   sweet bay   tupelo   slopes   scars   barbed wire
gallberry & briars   seedlings   blackjack oak   pitcher plants   bogs   cypress   scraped knees
absolute apartness   paucity   roots   archaic blooms   desiccated limbs   sinister   moonshine
twenty barrels of fermenting mash   four fifty-five gallon drums   seventy-five one gallon jugs
barbeque pits   alembics   penchants   dolors   broods   pittance   long gones   thickets
waxmyrtle & yaupon   generations   green canopy   water oaks & red oaks   watering holes
holly   red maple   yellow poplar   sassafras   redbay   square & round pointed shovels
sharpshooters   D grips   ditches   huckleberry   sourwood   dogwood   deer fly larvae
ambrosia beetles   born agains   apostasy   dampness   troves   common ground dove
hill country   fox squirrel   bobwhite quail   daybeams   rural hinterlands   gravel roads
rust   pitchfork   axes   stumps   bathtub planters   white sinks   good manners   fiddles   banjos
twelve strings   smithereens   cinder blocks   dismembers   adjoining   kinfolks   children
all grown up   feral life   reneges   rebels   clans   history   honeysuckle   Mardi Gras   revelers
beads & doubloons   beignets   red cups   arcana   hurricane force winds   dry ice   still eyes
pour over   matchstick forests   swathes   havoc   destruction   heaps   broken refrains
falling rains   surveyors   tracts   traces   brittle   loss   bad ways   ruin   floods   netherlands
crude   shortage   waves bending   riding it out   guts   praying   dread   distance   trespassers
water mocassin   rattlesnakes   burrows   gopher turtles   slimy salamanders   lizards   anoles
love bugs   wilderness   weeping willows   creosote posts   post hole diggers   ridges   dog days
cash crops   long rows   black soil   blackberry perseveres   hand-me-downs   sun strokes
sunshine   tough rows to hoe   rough terrain   a lost habitat   swifts   discernment   clouds
convergences   wild things   mockingbirds   fig trees   aluminum pie pans   threadbare quilts
kindred   wrens   nails   lumber   bream   trout   hushpuppies   catfish   pond dams   cole slaw
fishing holes   nests   cast of lines   planting   droppings   zeniths   stars   radiance   solstice
poultice   chiggers   mosquitoes   moth   toads   heedless   bullfrogs   branches   coachwhips
sliding   ill   heartworms   blackleg   nighthawks   aerie   martins   blooming   family plots
violets   cicada shedding   breaking out of shells   corrugated steel   pollen   nectar   nuances
sunbonnets   maples   buds   burgeoning   some occasional peacocks   cardinals   grosbeaks
yard art   blooming tire planters   those jockeys   atavisms   long tooth & short tooth rakes
acrimony   centipede grass   tracks   pickup trucks   Little Grey Fergies   family inheritances
obsolescence   brace & bits   crosscut saws   old harnesses   sharpening files   hammers
opossum   red fox   ice cream churns   butter churns   endurance   mud   raw wounds

dust in light beams   good riddances   roadkill   an overall angst-ridden sense of alienation
transgressive thoughts   desires & impulses   prostration   poaching   swear words   hell
coonhounds   dark nights   old courses   ruckus   ransacks   hollering   bib & brace overalls
yokels   briers   swamps   sweat   frays   drudging   strain   lichen   sloughing   fungi & algae
stupor   ticks   fleas   pleasure   tadpoles   ten pound test line   minnows   trotlines   barbs
polecats   red weeds   dock weeds   coffee weeds   soybean & cotton fields   pastures
settled & bothered   not to budge   stubborn sod   Cypress weed   right of ways
flickering heat & solitude   duress   insect-borne diseases   swallows of fire & venom
water & bone   thunder & lightning   empty hulls   crouching & trembling   sortilege
chicken feet   origins   family reunions   little bitties   pied-à-terre   scattered & collected
round & square bales   hayseed   hay strings   these parts   property lines   good fences
neighbors   vulnerability   gatherings   cuttings   depredation   leastways   landlocked
antediluvian   small hours   markings   trusses   headstones   small vistas   clearings
moldering   searching dreams   bowtie hubcaps   headlights   tailgates   mudgrips
self-possession   pine straw   fire   depth   a bare cross   migrations   moon colds
hoarded glass   herds   cuds   salt blocks   deep ruts   head gates   ear tags   banding tool
steers & heifers   stockyards   Brahma   Angus   Holstein   wee morning hours   bonfires
shrimp boats   blessings of the fleet   evenings   lost hours   horizon   least tern   nighttime
some peculiar things   countryside   county dumps   gentry   yeoman   equipoise   stands
hunter's orange   gauges & calibers   alone   relatives   breezes   foliage   shade   crickets
mortals   hubris   enclaves   abandonment   aestivation   shambled houses   salvage yards
heart pine planks   roadhouses   The River View Inn   broken spokes   shell middens
openhanded   nomenclature   catkins   swallows   bass   diamondbacks   indigo snakes
king snakes   sweet gums   water birch   herons   mallards   rambunctious   cavorting
festivals   high fallutting   beauty queens   foofaraw   football games   homecoming floats
donkey basketball   underdogs   mascots   hackles   rifles   screen porches   clotheslines
predilection   mien   red barns   scripturiency   dirt daubers   corbels   hip roofs   fascia
cinder blocks   maledictions   crawfish   perch   bait shops   muddy rivers   musings
back bays   planks   piers   fountainheads   artesian wells   natural springs   sandbars
canebrakes   barrier islands   sand gnats   backwaters   watersheds   riffles   outboards
moles   cane poles   rotten bayous   sit still   serendipity   pitcher plants   dragonflies
horn fly   yearlings   frailty   scrawniness   aches & pains   auction barns   abattoirs   hunger
burns   stills   feed sacks   hand buckets   languishing   sprucing up   thickets   carrion
rotting logs   split rail fences   stagnant waters   town squares   fire ants   briers & thorns
humus   blossoms   saplings   spring   swale   barrows   foundations   excrescence   mules
goats   courthouses   shotgun houses   beams   steeples   old school bells   pastoriums
Steep Hollow Baptist Church   deacons   prayer   haylofts   swaying   sorrow   cedar
misnomers   juniper groves   drought   clay   sieves   veins   argots   makeshifts   gravel pits
stray cats   puddles   gleaming   fallow soil   breech birth   comealongs   pangs   waning
acronychal   billows   barefooted   shallow puddles   dithering   concentric   omphalos
handmade   cousins   spare parts   eye lifting hills   cow patties   rickety steps   stuck keys
milky eyes   country mile   affray   mute   cower   sullen   ricocheting   rototillers   breaking
plows   contradictions   cultivars   tomato seeds   hothouse   planting eyes   cucumbers   beans
compost   potato salad   pickling lime   produce stands   boiled & roasted peanuts   spigots
bushel baskets   scarecrows   cobwebs   black widows   brown recluse   erosion   blight

drought   waylayings   watermelon   pea hulls   corn cobs   largess   silk & stamens   stalks
velvet beans   Infant of Prague   Knights of Columbus   chivalry   wingtips   war stories
fedoras   American Legion 677   heroes   corner slots   pool tables   roosting   chicken coops
cottontail rabbits   feral hogs   troughs   woodpiles   wisteria   azaleas   camellias   gardenias
hydrangea   geese & guinea   cacophony   northward cannons   chagrin   barrel horses
cannon bones & coffin bones   reins   crape myrtle   dutch clover   placid pastures   boodles
hay racks   bahia   bermuda   ryegrass   Cogongrass   invasive species   labor   profit & debt
pecan trees   prospects   high-strung son   Red Man Moist Snuff   spittoons   rattled & shaken
rickety   ramshackle   breakneck   breezeway   diurnal   gloom   meddlesome   ornery   snags
nervous wrecks   triple-thirteen   eight-twenty-four-twenty-four   sun up to sun down
prescribed fires   bottlebrush   fire towers   bent tins   coffee & chicory   yellowjackets
dung beetles   daddy long-legs   bumble bees   hornet nests   pine beetles   rolly pollies
slash pine   bush hogs   plow disc   blueberry bushes   pear trees   plum jelly   fig leaves
stereotypes   Luna moth   chrysalis   Crane Creek Baptist Church   Cockaigne   buckeye
American lady   swallowtail   mourning cloaks   coyote dens   pup songs   cypress knees
box elder   tenacity   nostalgia   confederates   crescent lands   wailing   din   ghosts
predators   raptors   family   quill   hummingbirds   august   bumpkins   crackers   hicks
chawbacon   chitlings   felicitous egrets   grasshoppers   praying mantis   dagger moth
mimic spiders   nemesis   wire mesh fences   Mercurochrome   remembering   trespasses
scrapes   retreats   seedlings   progenitors   the evening star   lilts   warbles   crescendos & trills
mockingbirds   redheaded woodpeckers   verdant woods   Shiloh Baptist Church   tenets
fundamentals   grease guns   lathes   forges   cheater bars   alligators   divinations
earthworms   rod & reels   hookworm   lazy & lethargic   branches & stems   dogwood
swamp maple   tupelo   holly   black cherry sassafras   wild turkeys   towhees   crows
kitchen gardens   soughing   goings on   jambalaya & étouffée   cheese grits   sweet tea
all you can eat meat & threes   cornbread   peach cobblers   meringue pies   banana pudding
scratch biscuits & sawmill gravy   fried chicken   pork & beans   Crisco cans   fatback
dinner on the ground   covered dishes   smoked mutton   Sunday dress   sermons
grok & afflatus   homilies   folklore   umpteen times   Lord's Supper   sword drills
verses & hymns   honeybees   baptizing   shame & guilt   Amazing Grace
swimming holes   rope swings   inner tubes   our Lord & our savior
revivals   lineaments   instilled & still
Jesus Christ.

Where could I go?   O where could I go?
Seeking a refuge for my soul.

Needing a friend to save me in the end.   O where could I go?

Where could I go but to the Lord.

I swallow blood & wait on my plucking up by roots   extirpations of an old house.

The wells of native waters on blood soil wait precipitate steps of settles of ethics & morals
by applying principles & interest of theology & memory & a torpor of miracle bushes cover

                                                vagrant holds of inevitable prophecy.

One of these days I'm gonna   be getting strong
                                                                    & drink of weariness.

Homestead acres hold secrets.

My ancestors were given an ecclesiastic stone in a box from a lady & they despised its value
& remained in a warren of gleaming white. Underneath there is a man who is better

a good man   who will vanquish his shadow from the face of land   who will overcome doubts
& unrighteous desires with reason   overcome greed with contentment
envy with benevolence   falsehood with truth   want with vigilance
                                                anger with serenity   strife with peace.

Underneath the myrtle is a cry of anguish   but I will grieve not   for water lies beneath me
                                                            & fresh ripe berries fall upon me

& I may eat & drink & cool mine eyes to burn eternal well & never run dry.   The one
                                                wilderness cries & so does his cousin.

Continual burning & repair to a well where fire is never extinguished.

I have held solitude in arid land of unconquered sun & rivers dry & wood petrified deep
                                                turbulent rivers of flesh & blood.

& I don't want to write a palimpsest.

I want to be where the green grass grows & watch my crops pop up in rows & still

                                                        I dream a highway
for I was raised at the highway junction   at the Y of fifty-three & six-o-three
where before I was born my momma bought her some acres & built her a barn & drove all
sixty something head straight down highway fifty-three & that was a long time ago
before we got all the traffic coming through like we do now. We got gravel trucks
up & down umpteen times a day. They come from Joe Cuevas's & Edwin Shaw's
pits. Joe will do anything to make a buck & Edwin's too lazy for real work.

My father don't like them selling gravel.   What you got when your soil is gone?
You got nothing but a hole in the ground.   You have to hold onto your place.

My father was born like a king. Heaven & loss is a redemption of sin.
O   I remember singing hymn number fifty-nine
My heav'nly home is bright & fair   Its glitt'ring tow'rs the sun outshine
I feel like traveling on.   I feel like traveling on.

Nor pain not death can enter there   That heav'nly mansion shall be mine
I feel like traveling on   I feel like traveling on. I feel like traveling on.

Not one of my fathers traveled on.
Wise men   lords   landed & fenced   around a thousand hills.

Their rows ran long. I honestly do not know how the kind of work done
                                                                                by men got done
except they had been grounded in belief
plumb tickled as reason got courage
cultivated acres & transformed
a vagary.

To plow is an act of will   to compel soil to come straight to the surface.

It takes a long time & starting early in morning & plowing must always be against the ground
                              gentle & constant. Incessant pressure to take hold & keep hold.

I drift downward into an age past brogans & denim & course flannel down to the wrist
                                                                                a middle busting
                                                                                down to clay
                                                                                breaking.

Our virgin woods so dense beyond the clearings.

They was there before us before our stands took root
                                                                before our hymns carried through limbs
                              before the stop of an organ pulled a gullet from sweet breaded zeal
& prayings of royal blood with another chorus of sound doctrine
there sings the priesthood of saints   soprano & alto   tenor & bass.

Here is an arrangement along a scale most eschew. I will not ignore a bruised heel
wrapped in linen & purple robes flowing pierced under tribunal red sky.
Nor vex with transubstantiation like pastoral immersion in the cold flow of Crane Creek
after revival in summer heat surrounded by pasture green   deep clay of trine elution.

Revelations could shelter on the tongue   tender prophets bring biscuits
                                                                                fried catfish & barbeque
                                                                                droughts & blights

greater than castings from a breaking of ears on a sacred day given to a storehouse   to be
                                                                                without shame

I am awaiting tendrils & cloven hooves & clover field crimson

I tell you: more divine than imaginings is loess of genesis & body.

There is always loss.
There is always loss.   Held cosset to ground heaven comes.

My grandmother remembers a lightning strike right on the road in front of her.
Now some say ain't no such things.   Gases of plant decay boil underneath
                                                ignite   & burn easy as creek bed sand.

I too often have pulled toward a stable trail of memory.   The forest here is mostly logged
pockets of quicksand are known by us
silt is often at hand in springs
& water is hard.
Buicks decay.

The house is dusted cobwebs & wrought iron beds.
Winter troughs surround.

Landless among brothers I have drafted into such unknown.
                                        I hear envy saw a two stroke ebbing into pine.

So I will tell you this.   I loathe the mill & the goddamned miller.
The woods are trees & trees are the woods & both are of one truth
                                        & they will encroach upon our clearings.

I remember county tractors mowing ditches up toward Poplarville & down toward Kiln.
They were not cutting grass   but holding forests to stands.   I tell you
                                        the unity of the land & our people
                                        means ordeal & temptation.

This temptation tempts & will make believe
                                it is best to labor forth into a redoubt of duty.

Uncle Soren says faith is namely this paradox: the single individual is higher than all.
                                                                I don't know.
Mostly I feel sorry for those county road crews. Those men mow those ditches
                                        forever & a day
                                        never will the woods stop
                                        so cry for they deserve tears.

I am obliged to restrain   for my faith has not fulfilled & will fail to countervail God.
But do not cry for me   cry for yourself   for what I become will not be abraded.

My grandfather knew constellations & they followed his tract & faith unites all life in passion
& faith unites all passion to speak only of a tragic strength

to prove a night of bright faith for its own sake.

My grandfather became higher than all who cannot be mediated
         & how he came into just how he remains in this land.

Uncle Soren once told me that one of his friends who lived even south of us said God
is blessed he needs nothing & next to him the wise man   he needs little.

We are native to a paltriness of life & have plucked blackberries
wild along fencerows & shaws & upon fallow land

              & blood flows from thorns as sweetness
       silver pots are tainted with purples of our royal produce & preserves.

So keep me where rich creams are poured into a deep bowl of soaked dumplings
             hide me in this shelter
             here our remnants are

for who keeps promises to be more sweet than clusters gathering.

Here is our unity created in hymns & similarities of holy timbers inside
         the tongue may flow suspended in mornings of only joy
          in long days of summer oscitancy & contumacy
           comes a flight toward remembered nectars.

Tis so sweet.   Tis so sweet.

For I have been nourished by hymns & I have held their bodies upon my tongue
              & tis so sweet

as sweet as the strength of honeycombs he drew from hives
as sweet as tobacco chewed & dabbed upon my arm when I followed him
            & I knew I ought not to.

I just so wanted to be brave & strong. He was never afraid of being stung
          & stings have always put me down.

What he always knew & what I have had a hard time learning a little sting is worth taking
          if you steal sweetness from that pain.

I remember the slow dripping of honeycombs from his hands.
I remember the drone of so many workers gathering the nectar of honeysuckle
          wild upon the fencerows.

& how my father swung into an underground nest with the bushhog

came rising a vespine hum

in the arousal of an open envelope

a colony with an appearance of charred paper.

& he slowed the tractor before he jumped & most kept following through the field
& my father swelled with toxins inflicted & came near death & days he hurt

& days he hurt.

So much is the ordinance of providence.

Uncle Paul used to say that we are pressed on every side by troubles

but we are not crushed & broken.

We are hunted down

but God never abandons us.

We get knocked down but we get up again & keep going. Through suffering
these bodies constantly share in death so that life may also be seen in our bodies.

A lot of people who never joined our family would say different. They would say our bodies
are so small against the fullness of pain

the stings of consciousness.

We all pray.

We all pass away.

These bodies come to nothing
as a mystery enters a juncture.

We go crossing a bridge when once a swift current was forded

to alight on clay graced & be swept by cold water

revealing a timber residuum of consummation.

So I cross one path with joy in suffering.
Through the hills of exploding hearts   a radiant man remains
home salts wounds to violence   like a county not named after surrounding pines
in an old & dark forrest   traces of hidden light   brought against powers of brokenness

as a spring tears soil open

& if there were no witnesses & no evidence we could ignore or dismiss any other story.

We know a prophet predicts a servant will rule a last day.
A day all peace with us fields witness to terrified birth long-awaited.   Behold:
moon tidings of joy to all people born this day & a swaddling sky filled glory-light
believes the long-awaited star & scepter that would predict everlasting exile years.

So ablution needs lambent light to indagate into steadfast apogee & descry our labors otiose.
Still I cannot repine with longanimity an onus wanders into its own ilk & kind.

I come to the fields alone while the dew is still on the berries & the sound I hear falling
on my ear is the sound of an empty field.   Empty as I am to fill
the promise of berry pulp & passing of blood from a pricking of a berry thorn to flesh
                              beginning to tremble right hard when it opens to the spirit.

Here I am   to fill a stainless pot & bleed & joy in an anfractuos journey.
Here I am   luminous & righteous born blood & evil thorns
to bleed as a virtuous workman   exposed to pricking & guilt & hindrance.
Here I am   I wait upon sustenance   & theophany.

I am prone to come at this point of grace with hunger & patience.
I am used to a harvest abounding in every good work.

The fields are calm full & fair for the workman upon the soil
                    on the gleaming hills of Mississippi stands   a vast sweetness of morning.

Come to the fields   sweet is the morning air
& our endeavors begin & cease & again begin slow   bring sadnesses in a rise & flow.

The world seems to lie before me like a land of dreams   so beautiful   so new.

Offerings of joy   love   light   certitude   peace help for pain   to prosper by grace
                                                    & so much reaping.

No dirt farmers could ever afford to leave land fallow with only themselves to depend upon
                              & pride in self-reliance & the produce of our labor.
I sure know that tradition   an inheritance past soil.

Uncle Ezra says image is more than idea   a cluster of fused ideas & endowed with energy.
But I think he's done fallen off his rocker.

I go back to the fields   to jubilees   to dowers of eloquence   to white sugar grains in red pulp
to black seeds in green rinds   to butter rinds   to stems with dead curls   to thumping
to placing straw perpendicular   to waiting for a turn   to a way to know ripeness.

I remember washing hands with pulp & eating hearts
washing my red hands & going back to a heat of work.

My father no longer lifted the burden of melon   but it was he who brought harvest.
His strength was enough to place seeds in the ground
                              though the weight of melons was too much to bear.

He tended his vines with cottonseed meal:
                    seven parts of nitrogen to build proteins & enzymes & chlorophyll & hormones

two parts of phosphorus for the metabolic process & root development
two parts of potassium to regulate photosynthesis.

The day of independence makes the melon farmer & some use ammonia to spur growth.
He did not.

These are the intercessions made:
seed planted on an incisive spring morning   beds of raised loam
furrows of labor   thinning beds   seed meal laid by & not upon.
There will be space for vines to cover. We will step carefully & hunt your predator.

The wise-blooded foe of singular desire.
How he comes & swipes his paw over the rinds   leaving marks   & rolls melons off the hill.

The cost of the coyote: drying rinds scraped to white & scars to remain.

Waiting in the fields is anti-freeze in a hubcap
ground meat full of treble hooks to be guttled.

O how I crave the death of wisdom in the fields of faith   & dream of bloodprints.
I'll be dog gone.

There must be rivers of wise blood for dream fulfillment   for the ravenous devour prey
plunder in the evening
make divinations

& leave nothing
for the morning

inward scatterings   & attacks on the ferocious shrewd   & innocent.

Farewell elders: I know wisdom will come among you & will not spare.
Do not take that you do not know   lest it add poverty & corrupt inside.

Inside the depths of the hollows is such a darkness we see prominent stars
as the protection of limbs reveals heavens   concealed by sunlight.

I tell you.
I don't know how to abide in the imbroglios of our quillets   & be content.

The ground demanding belief   Sough.
& belief deferring to experience.   Sough.

Into hollows water flows.
I remember clearing the last forty of new ground in midday heat.
I remember falling trees down to water flowing through branches.

I remember my father held his saw & idled.

I remember an axehead pyramid over his shoulder.

$$\text{I remember throwing my gloves to the gravel}$$
$$\text{walking to the edge of the culvert}$$
$$\text{arching into stagnant water}$$

first letters of words I never would have enough to write
looking straight through water to the clay.

Such were my isagogics of land.

A particulate filtering through   falling to floors of glassed water traced low to grace.

It ain't like this is a place worth   but I ain't got nowhere else to go.   Look
there's tree & there's leaves.

That leaf never wanted to go anywhere except down
                              & that tree never wanted to go anywhere except up.

So I am grateful for trails I have come upon & I have come to believe & to stand
                                        beyond knowledge & the gentle image.

I do not know any trails other than trails I know.

Many times we were told of the mercy & grace of doing nothing
                                        & still flows our demurrant blood.

Uncle J.D. used to say in his sermons   unless a man be enthralled   he never will be free
& I have always been enthralled by the little congregation of rustics
who brought me up in spiritual & material comfort.

I am enamored beyond the years I was given   but I too have been stuck in the dark mud
my boots left & right in humus   afraid

fast sinking into the bog of a little known land on which the traces of my steps fell exhausted
as perhaps the last pullulation of lumpen blood coagulates in soil lade with detritus
                                        my appurtenance of inheritance

& I am so besotted by this place in decay & decadence unbeknownst to a child
of disciples who saw surely & plainly   in the branches they found rotten-hearted
                                        their best complement
                                        & greatest abaisance.
So much is myth in the telling of a told story.

So much is measured beforehand to meet a present need except there be joined some good
provision for the seeds sprung up a supply necessary to stock for a dearth
upon the land & all the provision of bred.

As the soil weakens so does the blood.

Uncle Don used to say every night there are two families in the world
                                        those having much & those having little.

Uncle Wilbur used to say we would all die of thirst here at this wellside

but my uncles ain't never come into this house with food not on the stove for taking
& they ain't never not taken some such offering as gumbo & butter beans
ain't never come in from the fields & hung their work shirts to dry
on the nails in the power pole behind the wash room
& not been provided for.

Provisions needed as divine kenosis   ordained to us not seeing beforehand
                                so spit on the ground & make some mud with saliva
                                        put it to our eyes & to our mouths.

It bothers me some to know what is known   & what is not.

If we consider all things well we can see the marvelous: a saulee of sustenance.

We grow some good crops on this piece of land but once our land was pretty near worn
& washed away by the capital power of a staple & we were feeble in our realm
                                        of rhetoric & prosperity & bale.

Our arrogant spines failed to give reverence & led our blood desire.
                                        Back then we had plenty of land.

Now I am the last son of a farming family
my only inheritance is such a slight oracy.

Let me tell you.

One day my folks will find in freezer chests & pantry closets:

a quietus of deep provision   peace we so desperately have sought   shadows cast on the sun
by passing clouds   okra & tomatoes   turnips & collards & mustards   dark rings of beets
leg quarters   creamed corn   mayhaw jelly   fig preserves   strawberried figs   peach preserves
pickled watermelon rinds   pecan halves   homemade syrup from Joiner's Market   blueberries
field peas   yellow squash   Gulf shrimp   leftover gumbo   corked pepper jars   ground round

& t-bones   stew meat & oxtail from Fortenberry's   pickled cucumbers   unknown decades
of solace.

So we lived in these places & they carry our names:

                    Leetown Madison Bienville McNeill Nicholson Necaise
                    Carriere Purvis Gautier Milledgeville Vancleave Sumrall

& we settled into our toponymy & the tires rotted away & crops waited on rain
                                                    & dust trails passed.

We came to these hills & soon enough came from them.
We pressed together as sorghum pressed to syrup.

I have come to a place near back where I'm from & some old battles still carry on old roads.

A peach peddler under the shade of live oaks guarantees his produce to a wary buyer.
                                                    Red globes   he says.

There's a story behind that man just left   he says   as I look over the produce of his stand.
He wants to build forty-six houses on forty acres near here.
As long as I sit on the County Board I won't let that happen.
Baskets of peaches for six dollars & a bag of tomatoes for four
if you don't want to break a ten.

He comes by this stand & talks about growth   he says.
I tell him if he wants to talk about growth   he buys peaches.

Homegrown   he says.
Our trees sit back on the banks of Boley Creek & he points beyond the road
away from the white stand he has shuttered & lettered red with his offerings
                                                    of produce & preserves
& familiar remnants of a graceful economy
& gospelplated with licenses of his core truth   & witness:

Smile: God Loves You   God Is My Pilot   Jesus Is Lord   Jesus Is So Precious To Me
Don't Be Caught Dead Without Jesus   As My Life Got Tougher My Faith Got Stronger
In God We Trust   Speed Limit: Don't Drive Faster Than Your Guardian Angel Can Fly
Christians Aren't Perfect: Just Forgiven   When All Else Fails: Read The Directions
Jesus Christ: Your Key to Salvation   With God All Things Are Possible   Take God's Road
If You're Headed In The Wrong Direction: God Allows U-Turns   Buckle Up With Jesus
One Way: Jesus God Is Greater Than Any Problems I Have   Jesus Paid It All   Stop & Pray
Don't Wait For The Hearse To Take You To Church

He points past the deep yard he swears has gone to wilderness since they don't stock parts for his Snapper   past the strands of barb wire & the few head of Brahma

                                                                    past the tree line.
                                                                    & I leave blessed.

God go with you he says & I am grateful for his benisons & salvation of acres

                                                                    for I have no pluck.

My Uncle Amos always claimed
I am not a prophet   nor am I the son of a prophet   I am a herdsman   plucking wild figs

                                                        but his name called burdensome

burdensome to the restoration of obstinate tenets pitched on open dirt & he miserly observed

                                                                    until the rooster crowed

in the wake of mornings when an auger bringing up soil catches a tuft of cloth

                                                                    & brings in flesh
in the wake of ribs soft between a steer & corral boards breaking as deep breath

                                                                    against a skull
in the wake of mornings when bales are brought from dry fields & sons sit high upon stacks

                                                                    of labor & fall.

We are a hidebound people   & an auger will draw us to soil
                                                        & a board will break on our backs
                                                        & our sons will fall in the fields of hay

& we remain   a remnant on these traces.

Next to my kin is my parcel:
Hancock County, Mississippi.

North one-half of the Northeast one-fourth of section 17 township 5 South range 14 West
South 59 degrees 39 minutes 23 seconds west 188.85 feet   thence South 61 degrees 25
minutes 33 seconds West 155.91 feet   thence South 69 degrees 49 minutes 08 second West
75.53 feet   thence South 76 degrees 53 minutes 24 seconds West 177.61 feet   thence leaving
said margin   North 00 degrees 04 minutes 36 seconds West 236.32 feet to a 4" post
thence East 544.09 feet for the point of beginning.

The Benedictory Pastoral

Pastoral [Blessed is the father]

after revelations

Blessed is the father who sleeps with gospel upon a lightered chest   who keeps his word
                    upon onionskin
he shall tear awake strictures of blood & his heart shall stop by peens of unprest water.

Blessed is the father who passes among the pews   who shakes his wingtips toward God
                     he offers resin
as a remnant from his labor   for his son shall write in aphorisms broken & dark as myrrh.

Blessed is the father whose garments dry upon nails   whose flesh holds the soil of fields
                    he tends a vine
green & free of blight & he shall harvest fruits open with pure crystals of sweet pudor.

Blessed is the father who eats dinner on the ground   who sits on roots of noonday shade
                    he shall reign
& this ordinant future shall pass in a sclerosis of tracts & at the table he will take supper.

Blessed is the father who raises biscuits in iron skillets   who pours grits like molten lead
                  in early morning
he offers a fine roux for tomato & resurrection   & over his son days will have no power.

Blessed is the father who keeps the way   offers no brag or big   talk he shall keep his word
                  redeem our ruin
among murmell people   he will roll his sleeves & his deeds shall burn as heartwood tinder.

Blessed is the father who offers cottonseed meal   & offers summer refection in harsh lands
                  in a generation
his vines shall grow lax & graceful   & in early morning harvest he shall have right to enter.

Acknowledgements

Grateful acknowledgment is made to the editors of the following publications where some of these poems first appeared, sometimes with different titles or in slightly different form:

2 Bridges Review — "Pastoral [O fall down barn]"

Alice Blue Review — "Pastoral [Amen rises amid pales]," "Pastoral [Among bales I crawl]," "Pastoral [Hunger raddles]," "Pastoral [We threw roots into fire]"

Anti- — "Augur of Cleavage"

Colorado Review — "Pastoral [Saplings fall under axe]"

Country Music — "Pastoral [So cast back to an old place]," "Pastoral [The violence of lightning striking pine]"

Cream City Review — "Pastoral [In the bright falling]"

Denver Quarterly — "Augur of Forest for Trees," "Augur of Principle"

Free Verse — "Augur of Flailing," "Augur of Wright"

Grist — "Pastoral [Amidst ashes]"

Gulf Stream — "Pastoral [Blessed is the father]"

H_NGM_N — "Pastoral [Deep within the ravine]"

Hobble Creek Review — "Pastoral [I always find myself over yonder]"

Kenyon Review — "Pastoral [A stubborn roan lows]"

Rock & Sling — "Pastoral [On hazy mornings]"

Sandhill Review — "Pastoral [This entire most beautiful order]"

Third Coast — "Augur of Illuminated Manuscript"

Toad Suck Review — "Pastoral [So great a debtor]"

Tusculum Review — "Augur of Ash," "Augur of Begottenness," "Augur of Deep Wells," "Augur of Pines," "Pastoral [Falling among beams]," "Pastoral [God must rather bushhog]"

Washington Square — "Pastoral [Glorious body drawn from fields]"

Selections from "The Heart Pine Prophecy" were published in *Denver Quarterly*, *Horse Less Review* & *Tupelo Quarterly*.

The Saw Year Prophecies was published as a chapbook by Slash Pine Press.

About the Author

Brent House grew up in Necaise, Mississippi, where he raised cattle and watermelons with his father. His poems have appeared in *Kenyon Review*, *Third Coast*, and *Denver Quarterly*, among other publications, and they appear regularly in *The Tusculum Review*, where he serves as a contributing editor. He received his MFA from Georgia College in Milledgeville.

www.ingramcontent.com/pod-product-compliance
Lightning Source LLC
Chambersburg PA
CBHW081339120626
46546CB00011B/3420